The

Renassance
Their Story and
Legacy

Author/Illustrator

TONY R. SMITH

Table of contents

History of the Harlem Renaissance

The Harlem Renaissance was a period of intense intellectual and cultural activity in African American communities of New York City. It is sometimes called the Black Renaissance, but that term also has other connotations unrelated to the Harlem Era. The name arose because the authors and artists who flourished during the period tended to come from the more affluent neighborhoods of Harlem within the borough of Manhattan. Some historians cite it as beginning in 1916 with the publication of W E B Du Bois' article "The Prose and Poetry of Africa" in Crisis magazine, though some point to recent research showing its roots go back as far as 1919. The first book-length publication on this subject, however, appeared only in 1982 by Henry Louis Gates Jr., himself a participant in many early black literary circles, under the title The African American Century: An Essay on Race in America.

Overview of the Harlem Renaissance

The Harlem Renaissance was a time of extraordinary scholarly and social movement in African American people group of New York City. It is once in a while called the Harlem Renaissance; however that term likewise has different implications irrelevant to the Harlem Period. The name emerged on the grounds that the creators and specialists who prospered during the period would in general come from the more rich neighborhoods of Harlem inside the district of Manhattan. A few history specialists refer to it as starting in 1916 with the distribution of W E B Du Bois' Composition and Verse of Africa" in Emergency magazine, however a highlight late exploration showing its foundations return similarly as 1919. The primary book-length distribution regarding this matter, in any case, showed up just in 1982 by Henry Louis Gates,Jr., himself a member in many early dark scholarly circles, under the title The African American Hundred years: A Paper on Race in America .

Writers of the Harlem Renaissance

The Harlem Renaissance was a time in African American history when African Americans experienced their greatest cultural and intellectual flowering. Some of the most important writers during this period were Claude McKay, Zora Neale Hurston, Langston Hughes, Henry Lewis Gates, Jr., Countee Cullen, Alain Locke, Richard Wright, and Jean Toomer.

Artists of the Harlem Renaissance

An important development of the Harlem Renaissance was that many African American artists and writers sought to break free from the confines of social conventions and stereotypes. They sought to create an artistic identity that would be uniquely their own. This creative movement continued into the 1920s, with a general focus on black artists and writers, but also including Native Americans, Mexican Americans, and Asian Americans.

The Harlem Renaissance in music and dance

In both the cultural and economic arenas, the Harlem Renaissance was a crucial turning point in African American history. The Harlem Renaissance is most often associated with the literary, political, and artistic movements that emerged in African American communities of New York City during the 1920s. However, its importance extends beyond this period to the present day because it marked a shift in thought within African Americans from an identity based on their race to one based on their culture.

Impact of the Harlem Renaissance

The Harlem Renaissance had an enormous impact on African American culture, which was further enhanced by the establishment of cultural institutions such as the Schomburg Center for Research in Black Culture. The movement brought together black social activists and intellectuals, and helped create new opportunities in publishing and other fields. Other cultural transformations were also afoot, including jazz, which would later be known as "black music"; films such as The Birth of a Nation; the emergence of literary journals such as Opportunity, Crisis and New Negro; the creation of the first black women's colleges (Amherst, Fisk and others); the founding of new secular organizations such as the NAACP; a renewed interest in African cultures; increased activism in support of racial equality; and much more.

Some important figures from the period after the end of the Harlem Renaissance

Although the Harlem Renaissance was essentially over by 1940, not all the changes that were introduced were permanent. Some of them were altered or reversed during the civil rights era, with an important exception in the case of jazz. The Harlem Renaissance started to decline in the early 1930s and ended for a variety of reasons, including the Great Depression and World War II. Some important figures from this period after the end of the Harlem Renaissance are: W E B Du Bois, Langston Hughes, Marian Anderson, Countee Cullen, Josephine Baker, Duke Ellington, and Miles Davis.

The Harlem Renaissance is one of the most important periods in African American history, and one of the most influential movements in US history. The Harlem Renaissance was a cultural movement that took place in Harlem, New York City, from about the 1920s through to the 1950s. It was a brief period of African American cultural and political history with a series of cultural innovations in literature, music, art, architecture, religion, and social activism.

When was the Harlem Renaissance?

The Harlem Renaissance was a period of intense intellectual and cultural activity in African American communities of New York City. It is sometimes called the Black Renaissance, but that term also has other connotations unrelated to the Harlem Era. The name arose because the authors and artists who flourished during the period tended to come from the more affluent neighborhoods of Harlem within the borough of Manhattan. Some historians cite it as beginning in 1916 with the publication of W E B Du Bois' article "The Prose and Poetry of Africa" in Crisis magazine, though some point to recent reunions of black intellectuals as marking at least a partial beginning. The 1920s saw a proliferation of black-owned magazines, including NAACP Publications and The Noble Ebony that published short stories, essays, poems and book reviews by authors such as Langston Hughes, Countee Cullen, Nella Larsen and Wallace Thurman. African American Facebooks such as Opportunity and The Negro Digest included parts on literature and culture. Similarly groundbreaking were Katherine Johnson's Nella Larsona c 1941 Pacesetter Books series on African American culture. Some events marking the Harlem Renaissance include: • May 16–20, 1925: National Urban League Conference on Race Relations held in Atlantic City, New Jersey. • July 17–21 1925: 3rd World Congress of Representative Women (WCW) held in Chicago, Illinois. The WCW established International Woman Suffrage Alliance to bring together all countries for international collaboration on women's rights issues. • October 1929: Harlem book fair inaugurated at 25th Street and Seventh Avenue with support from city government • 1930: Sculpture exhibit "The 10 Faces Of Africa" by Marcus Garvey appears at Armory Show in NYC • 1936: Langston Hughes begins his work at freelance writing career with John Strachan at Peacock Run Press in NYC • 1937: Playwright Lorraine Hansberry first produced 'A Raisin In the Sun' at HEREFORDSOUND THEATER • October 1938: Official celebration of New York City becoming a 'Negro City' takes place with speeches by Mayor Fiorello LaGuardia and Mayor Jimmy Walker.

Who were some of the authors and artists during the Harlem Renaissance?

The Harlem Renaissance was a period of intense intellectual and cultural activity in African American communities of New York City. It is sometimes called the Black Renaissance, but that term also has other connotations unrelated to the Harlem Era. The name arose because the authors and artists who flourished during the period tended to come from the more affluent neighborhoods of Harlem within the borough of Manhattan. Some historians cite it as beginning in 1916 with the publication of W E B Du Bois' article "The Prose and Poetry of Africa" in Crisis magazine, though some point to recent research which suggests it began between 1912 and 1918. No matter when it began, it was a creative time at the heart of black culture in America, when writers and poets like Claude McKay, Langston Hughes, James Weldon Johnson, and Zora Neale Hurston created some of their most astonishing work.

What were some of the major themes of the Harlem Renaissance?

The Harlem Renaissance was a moment in time during the 20th century when African Americans collectively became empowered, self-aware and proud of whom they were. A period of intense intellectual and cultural activity took place amongst African American communities in New York City. The Harlem Renaissance was a time with many artistic, literary, and musical milestones to celebrate. The Harlem Renaissance began around 1916 with the publication of W.E.B Du Bois' article "The Prose and Poetry of Africa" in Crisis magazine. From 1916-1925 authors and artists flourished in Harlem centering more on the intellectual community rather than artists who were well established prior to the period's onset such as Claude McKay, McKay later known as simply 'Mckay'. Another celebrated artist is Langston Hughes who wrote notable novels like "The Big Sea", "Scribner's as well as Blues lyrics such as "Joe Hill", "Strange Fruit" among many others that established him as an artist for life. Another art form that flourished in the Harlem Renaissance was Dadaism which consisted of a group of post-impressionists poets who were influenced by African American Folklore such as Charles Bukowski (Beryl Williams), Kenneth Koch (Henry Louis Gates).There were also many jazz greats during the Harlem Renaissance including Bessie Smith vocalist and record breaker with her songs like "Baby Please Don't Go", "Crazy Blues" among many others as well as Louis Armstrong saxophonist who recorded his famous song

"When you're Smiling And Happy and when your head hangs low... that is how I Know you are Thinking Of Me" A very important landmark in early 20th century African American literature was Langston Hughes producing his famous novels like, The Big Sea; The Blacker the Berry; A Dream Deferred among others as well as jazz poet Kenneth Koch whose work included poetry book named All Souls Rising (All Souls Rising) among many others which are all Nobel Laurette Examples Of 20th Century Literature.

Extraordinary Relocation Period

The northern Manhattan neighborhood of Harlem was intended to be a high society white area during the 1880s, however fast overdevelopment prompted void structures and frantic landowners trying to fill them. In the mid-1900s, a couple of working class Dark families from one more area known as Dark Bohemia moved to Harlem, and other Dark families followed. A few white occupants at first battled to keep African Americans out of the area, however bombing that many whites in the end escaped.

Outside factors prompted a populace blast: From 1910 to 1920, African American populaces relocated in enormous numbers from the South toward the North, with conspicuous figures like W.E.B. Du Bois driving what became known as the Incomparable Relocation. In 1915 and

1916, catastrophic events in the south put Dark laborers and tenant farmers unemployed. Moreover, during and after The Second Great War, movement to the US fell, and northern scouts traveled south to tempt Dark specialists to their organizations. By 1920, approximately 300,000 African Americans from the South had moved north, and Harlem was one of the most famous objections for these families.

This significant populace shift brought about a Dark Pride development with pioneers like Du Bois attempting to guarantee that Dark Americans got the credit they merited for social everyday issues. Two of the earliest forward leaps were in verse, with Claude McKay's assortment Harlem Shadows in 1922 and Jean Toomer's Stick in 1923. Social liberties

dissident James Weldon Johnson's The Personal history of An Ex-Shaded Man in 1912, trailed by God's Trombones in 1927, transformed the universe of fiction.

Writer and du Bois and Jessie Redmon Fauset's 1924 novel There Is Disarray investigated Dark Americans tracking down a social character in a white-overwhelmed Manhattan. Fauset was scholarly manager of the NAACP magazine The Emergency and fostered a magazine for Dark youngsters with Du Bois.

Humanist Charles Spurgeon Johnson, who was fundamental in molding the Harlem scholarly scene, utilized the presentation party for There Is Disarray to sort out assets to set out Freedom, the Public Metropolitan Association magazine he established and altered a triumph that reinforced journalists like Langston Hughes. Hughes was at that party alongside other promising Dark essayists and editors, as well as strong white New York distributing figures. Before long numerous essayists found their work showing up in standard magazines like Harper's.

Zora Neale Hurston

Anthropologist and folklorist Zora Neale Hurston pursued discussion through her contribution with a distribution called FIRE!! Helmed by white writer and Harlem authors' benefactor Carl Van Vechten and loaded up with works from productive Dark scholars including Langston Hughes, Zora Neale Hurston and Aaron Douglas, the magazine eroticized the existences of Harlem inhabitants. Van Vechten's past fiction worked up interest among whites to visit Harlem and exploit the way of life and nightlife there. However Van Vechten's work was denounced by more seasoned illuminating presences like DuBois, it was embraced by Hurston, Hughes and others.

Countee Cullen

Verse, as well, thrived during the Harlem Renaissance. Countee Cullen was 15 when he moved into the Harlem home of Reverend Frederick A. Cullen, the minister of Harlem's biggest assemblage, in 1918. The area and its way of life illuminated his verse, and as an undergrad at New York College, he got prizes in various verse challenges prior to going onto Harvard's lords program and distributing his most memorable volume of verse: Variety. He followed it up with Copper Sun and The Melody of the Earthy colored Young lady, and proceeded to compose plays as well as kids' books.

Cullen got Guggenheim cooperation for his verse in and wedded Nina Yolande, the little girl of W.E.B. DuBois. Their wedding was a significant get-together in Harlem. Cullen's surveys for Opportunity magazine, which ran under the section "Dull Pinnacle," zeroed in on works from the African-American literati and covered the absolute greatest names of the age.

Louis Armstrong

The music that permeated in and afterward blast out of Harlem during the 1920s was jazz, frequently played at speakeasies offering unlawful alcohol. Jazz turned into an extraordinary draw for Harlem inhabitants, however outside white crowds moreover.

The Harlem Renaissance was one of the most influential eras in American history. The cultural, social, and artistic movement had a profound impact on African-American culture and beyond.

But what made the Harlem Renaissance such a monumental moment in history? In this section, we explore the reasons why the Harlem Renaissance was so important and its lasting impact on American culture today. We discuss the various aspects of the movement, from literature and music to the social and political changes that it brought about. We also examine how the Harlem Renaissance was a turning point for African-Americans' struggle for equality and freedom, and why it continues to resonate with so many today. Through this article, we will explore why the Harlem Renaissance made such a meaningful difference, and how its legacy still impacts our culture today.

Overview of the Harlem Renaissance

The Harlem Renaissance was an important period of African-American culture, art, and literature. It was a time when African-American artists and writers were challenging the status quo, exploring new ideas, and pushing the boundaries of art. It was also a time when the African-American community was gaining visibility, and standing up for their rights and freedoms.

The Harlem Renaissance was important for a variety of reasons. It was a period of self-expression and creativity, where African-American artists, writers, and musicians could explore and express their unique experiences and perspectives. It also challenged the oppressive and racist systems of the time, and gave African-Americans a platform to speak out, demonstrate, and fight for their rights. The Harlem Renaissance also demonstrated a new level of cultural, economic, and political power among African-Americans. It provided a sense of pride and unity among African-American communities and gave them a voice to demand equal rights.

The Harlem Renaissance is still considered one of the most important periods of African-American history, and its legacy continues to influence our culture today. Its impact on literature, music and the arts is undeniable, and it stands as a testament to the power of creativity and self-expression. The Harlem Renaissance also helped to create a sense of solidarity and empowerment among African-Americans and played an important role in the fight for civil rights. The lasting impact of the Harlem Renaissance is seen in our culture today, and its importance cannot be overstated.

The Influence of Music and Literature in the Harlem Renaissance

One of the most important components of the Harlem Renaissance was its influence on literature and music. Writers and poets such as Langston Hughes, Zora Neale Hurston, and Countee Cullen wrote about topics that were often considered taboo, from racial identity and politics to the spiritual aspects of African-American life. Through their works, they highlighted the struggles and triumphs of African-Americans, as well as the importance of preserving their heritage and culture.

Meanwhile, musicians such as Duke Ellington, Louis Armstrong, and Jelly Roll Morton created a new style of music that was heavily influenced by the African-American community. This music, known as jazz, served as an expression of freedom and creativity, and it helped to bridge the gap between African-American and mainstream American culture. It also helped to bring African-American music to the forefront of American culture.

The literature and music of the Harlem Renaissance was a major catalyst for positive social and political change, as they helped to spark conversations about race, equality, and freedom. By highlighting the unique aspects of African-American life and culture, the Harlem Renaissance had a lasting impact on how African-Americans were viewed and treated in America. This influence can still be seen today, as the works of writers and musicians from the Harlem Renaissance continue to inspire and influence new generations of African-American and other minority artists.

Artistic Contributions of the Harlem Renaissance

The Harlem Renaissance was one of the most influential eras in American history. It was a cultural, social, and artistic movement that has had a profound impact on African-American culture and beyond. Several artists, writers, and musicians of the time helped to shape the unique character of the Harlem Renaissance

Artists such as painter Aaron Douglas, sculptor Augusta Savage, and photographer James Van Der Zee were some of the movers and shakers of the era. Their work served to capture the spirit of

African-American life and culture. Their art was a reflection of the struggles and achievements of African-Americans and provided an inspiring glimpse into the potential of a people who had been marginalized and oppressed for centuries.

The Harlem Renaissance's influence on literature was even more impactful. Writers such as Langston Hughes, Claude McKay, and Zora Neale Hurston became some of the most iconic figures of the era and their works highlighted the beauty and power of African-American culture. Through their art, they promoted themes of racial pride and equality, helping to reshape the narrative of African-American life and inspiring generations to come.

The Harlem Renaissance was a pivotal moment for African-Americans when their talents and contributions were finally acknowledged and celebrated. It was a period of artistic and intellectual creativity that brought about social change and helped to shape the American culture we know today. The lasting impact of the Harlem Renaissance is still seen in many aspects of our lives, from music and literature to politics and the way that African-Americans are perceived and treated.

Social Impact of the Harlem Renaissance

The Harlem Renaissance was an incredibly impactful moment in American history. It changed the landscape of African-American culture and history forever, and its legacy has continued to reverberate through our culture to this day. The movement was a powerful combination of literature, music, art, and social and political change that changed the way African-Americans were viewed and treated in society.

The Harlem Renaissance marked the first time African-Americans were given a voice and a platform to express their views and opinions. This was critical in changing how African-Americans were viewed, as it was the first time African-American culture and art were celebrated and appreciated by the mainstream public. This allowed for the emergence of powerful African-American poets, writers, painters, and musicians who were finally allowed to share their stories and perspectives with the world.

The Harlem Renaissance also had a profound impact on the social and political climate of the time. The fight for civil rights and equality gained traction during this period, and the movement laid the groundwork for the civil rights movement of the 1950s and 1960s. The Harlem Renaissance was an important step in bringing about the fight for African-American equality, and its legacy is still felt today. The movement showed the world that African-Americans had a voice and were capable of making a difference, and its influence can be seen in the fight for social justice and civil rights today.

The Political Impact of the Harlem Renaissance

The Harlem Renaissance was a crucial period in American history that revolutionized African-American culture and society. This period, beginning in the 1920s and ending in the 1940s, saw an explosion of creativity and expression among African-Americans living in the United States. This period was a turning point in the struggle for racial equality and civil rights. It is credited with inspiring generations of African-Americans to fight against racism and injustices.

The Harlem Renaissance was a major contribution to the fight for equality. It acted as a catalyst for the civil rights movement in the United States, helping to bring attention to the struggles of African-Americans and inspiring them to push for change through art, literature, music, and political activism. During this era, African-Americans were able to express their culture and identity through art, literature, and music. This was a crucial moment for African-Americans to be able to express themselves in a way that was not allowed before. Furthermore, the Harlem Renaissance also brought attention to the plight of African-Americans and helped bring to the forefront their struggles for civil rights and equality.

The Harlem Renaissance was an important movement in American history, one that helped brings to light the struggles faced by African-Americans and helped to bring about positive changes in the fight for equality and civil rights. Through its various forms of expression, the Harlem Renaissance provided an outlet for African-Americans to express themselves and helped to empower them in their fight for justice. The Harlem Renaissance also left a lasting impact on American society and culture to this day, as its legacy of activism and art is still echoed in our culture today.

The Legacy of the Harlem Renaissance

The Harlem Renaissance was a pivotal time in American history when African-Americans began to take greater ownership of their culture and make their presence known in society. The cultural and artistic movement was an expression of their identity and a push for equality and civil rights. This era saw the rise of influential authors, musicians, visual artists, and activists. Writers such as Langston Hughes, Zora Neale Hurston, and W.E.B. Du Bois provided African-Americans with a literary platform through which they could express themselves and tell their stories. Musicians such as Louis Armstrong, Duke Ellington, and Bessie Smith created the distinct sound of jazz and blues music, while visual artists such as Aaron Douglas and Augusta Savage depicted African-American life and culture in a vivid and meaningful way. In addition, activists such as Marcus Garvey and A. Philip Randolph led the civil rights movement, advocating for equal rights and opportunities for African-Americans.

The Harlem Renaissance also saw the emergence of a unique African-American identity and culture that helped to shift the perception of African-

Americans in American society. The movement also helped to solidify African-Americans' presence in the arts, music, and literature and laid the groundwork for future generations of African-Americans to continue to make strides in those fields. The Harlem Renaissance also provided a platform for African-Americans to make their voices heard in the political arena and helped to spur the civil rights movement. The Harlem Renaissance thus stands as a major milestone in American history, as well as a lasting legacy for African-Americans today.

The Role of African-American Women in the Harlem Renaissance

One of the most vital factors in the success of the Harlem Renaissance was the role of African-American women. Throughout the movement, African-American women made a significant contribution to literature, music, art, and politics.

African-American women such as Zora Neale Hurston, Jessie Redmon Fauset, and Nella Larsen, among others, made invaluable contributions to the literary scene during the Harlem Renaissance. Their works explored a variety of topics, from black womanhood to the injustices of racism, and opened the door for a new wave of African-American literature.

The music scene was also heavily influenced by African-American women. Bessie Smith, Ethel Waters, and Ma Rainey were some of the most popular female blues singers of the time, and their performances helped to bring the blues to a wider audience. African-American female musicians were also influential in introducing jazz, swing, and gospel music to the world.

The Harlem Renaissance was also a major force in the struggle for African-American civil rights and social justice. African-American women such as Mary McLeod Bethune, Mary Church Terrell, and Sarah Louise Delany, among others, were all involved in various social movements and organizations. Through their advocacy, African-American women played an important role in pushing for equal rights, education reform, and the passage of anti-lynching laws.

The Role of African-American women in the Harlem Renaissance was essential in ushering in a new era of cultural, social, and political progress.

Their contributions to literature, music, and activism opened the door for a new wave of African-American creativity and progress. To this day, the legacy of the Harlem Renaissance continues to impact American culture, and African-American women still serve as vital voices in the struggle for equality and justice.

The Impact of the Harlem Renaissance on American Culture Today

The Harlem Renaissance was a vibrant period in American history, and it had an immense impact on the nation's culture and society. It was a period of artistic and literary expression, which provided a platform for African-Americans to share their stories and experience in an environment that was often hostile to them. During this time, African-American literature, art, and music flourished, creating a unique and powerful cultural movement. Furthermore, the Harlem Renaissance marked a turning point in the African-American struggle for social and political equality. The movement provided a platform for African-Americans to express their views and ideas, and the period saw the emergence of influential writers, musicians, and artists such as Langston Hughes, Zora Neale Hurston, and Louis Armstrong.

The impact of the Harlem Renaissance is still felt today. Its legacy is evident in the works of contemporary artists, writers, and musicians who are inspired by the movement. The movement also had a political impact, inspiring people from all backgrounds to push for greater civil rights and social justice. Furthermore, the movement helped create a sense of pride in African-American culture and heritage, which has continued to grow and evolve over the years. The Harlem Renaissance was an incredibly important era in American history, and its influence can still be felt today.

How the Harlem Renaissance Changed the Perception of African-Americans

The Harlem Renaissance was a transformative era in American history. From the 1920s to the 1930s, this cultural, social, and artistic movement brought tremendous changes in the cultural landscape and was an influential force in the struggles of African-Americans for racial equality and freedom. Artists and writers such as Zora Neale Hurston, Langston Hughes, and Countee Cullen used their art and literature to express the African-American experience and to challenge racial stereotypes. The vibrant music of jazz and blues became a major part of the Harlem Renaissance and brought African-American music to the mainstream. The Harlem Renaissance also sparked a new sense of self-confidence and pride in African-American culture and an awareness of their shared heritage and history.

The Harlem Renaissance changed the perception of African-Americans and their place in American society. For the first time, African-Americans were seen as vibrant and creative people, rather than an inferior race. The Harlem Renaissance made clear the power of African-American art, culture, and music, and how African-American art, culture, and music could impact other cultures and be appreciated by the mainstream. Furthermore, the Harlem Renaissance allowed African-Americans to express their voices and experiences in literature, music, and art for the first time. The Harlem Renaissance was, and still is, a symbol of hope, progress, and freedom for African-Americans and its legacy continues to echo in our culture today.

The Significance of Langston Hughes and the Harlem Renaissance

The Harlem Renaissance was a major cultural, social and artistic movement that had a lasting influence on African-American culture and beyond. It was a period of tremendous creative and intellectual growth and a time when African-American culture was celebrated and explored in depth. The movement was largely fueled by the work of writer, poet, and activist Langston Hughes, who helped to solidify the movement's message and reach. Hughes's work helped to define and inspire a new generation of African-Americans, and provided a platform for them to express their unique view of the world.

Hughes's work was also a major part of the movement's political agenda. His work was often deeply critical of the status quo, and often highlighted the injustices that were faced by African-Americans. Hughes and other members of the Harlem Renaissance sought to use their art to draw attention to the struggles African-Americans faced in a segregated society. Through their work, they aimed to achieve social and political change.

The Harlem Renaissance was a watershed moment in American history, and its influence can be felt to this day. It was a time when African-Americans were finally able to fully express their culture and identity. The work of Langston Hughes and other members of the movement continue to resonate, and their legacy is a lasting reminder of the importance of cultural expression. The Harlem Renaissance is a symbol of the power of art to inspire change and motivate people to fight for a better future.

The Enduring Legacy of the Harlem Renaissance

The Harlem Renaissance, also known as the "New Negro Movement" of the 1920s, was a transformative period in African-American history. It was a time of great cultural, social, and political change for African Americans. With the influx of African-Americans to larger cities such as New York and Chicago, a new African-American identity began to take shape. Writers such as Langston Hughes, Countee Cullen, and Zora Neale Hurston were among the most prominent authors of the period, and their works helped define the Harlem Renaissance. Jazz music flourished in this era, as musicians such as Louis Armstrong, Duke

Ellington, and Cab Calloway revolutionized the sound of American music.

The Harlem Renaissance was also an important period for African-American activism and political consciousness. Activists such as W.E.B. Du Bois, Marcus Garvey, and Ida B. Wells-Barnett were major figures in the fight for civil rights and social justice. They championed a new generation of African-Americans who sought to challenge the status quo and push for greater equality and freedom. This period also saw the rise of the "New Negro" philosophy, which encouraged African-Americans to embrace their culture and identity and to resist racism and prejudice.

Today, the legacy of the Harlem Renaissance remains alive and vibrant. Its influence can be seen in the works of writers, musicians, and activists of all backgrounds. Its spirit of creativity, resistance, and resilience continues to inspire people to make a difference in their communities and the world. The Harlem Renaissance was an important period in history, not only for African-Americans but for all people. Its legacy will continue to resonate for generations to come.

Learn

All 50 US States

And Capitals

Learn All 50 States and Capitals

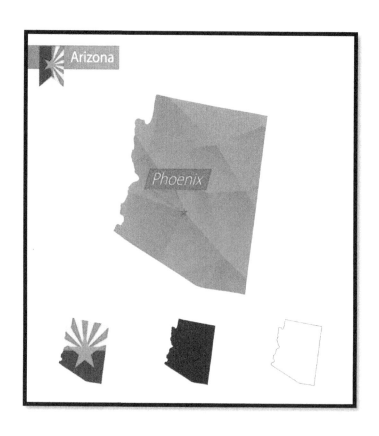

54

Arkansas

Little Rock

ARKANSAS

California

Sacramento

56

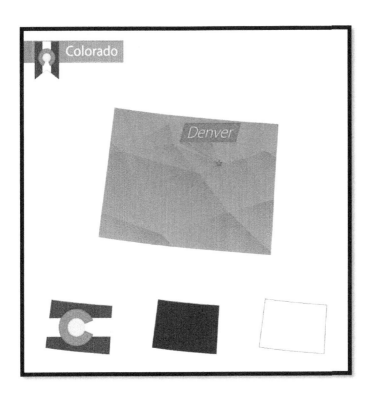

57

Connecticut

Hartford

58

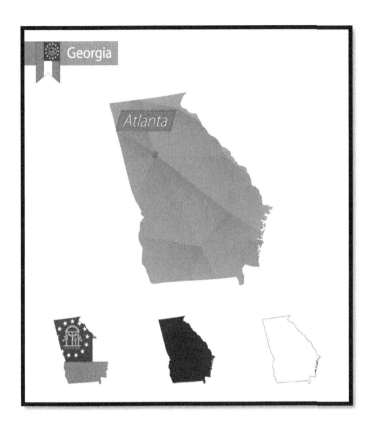

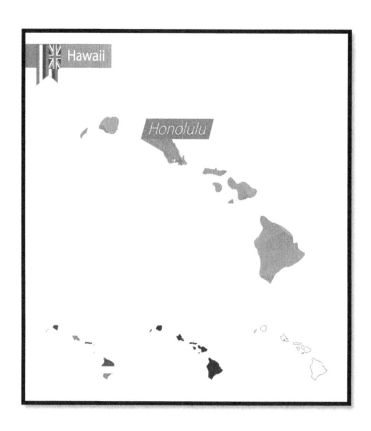

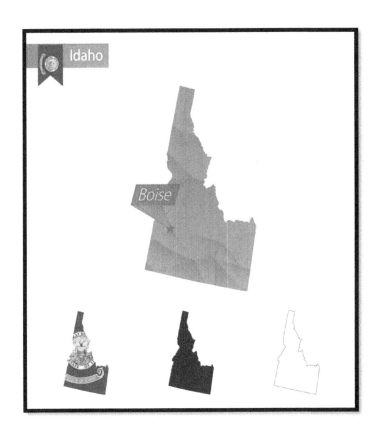

Idaho

Boise

Illinois

Springfield

64

Indiana

Indianapolis

Kansas

Topeka

KANSAS

Maine

Augusta

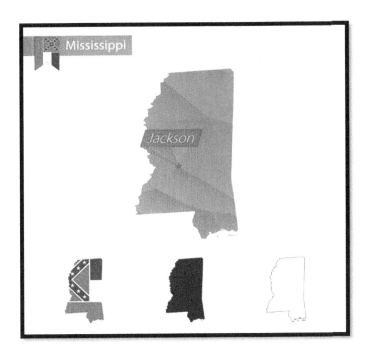

Mississippi

Jackson

Missouri

Jefferson City

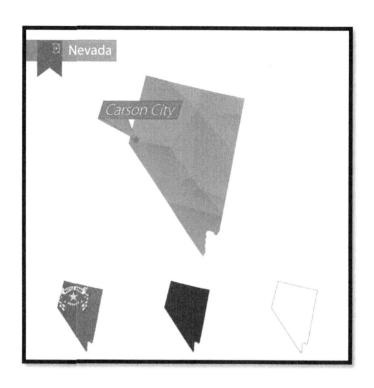

Concord

New Jersey

Trenton

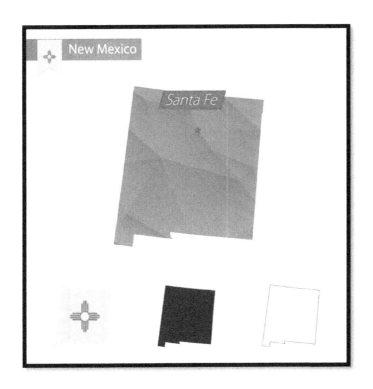

New Mexico

Santa Fe

81

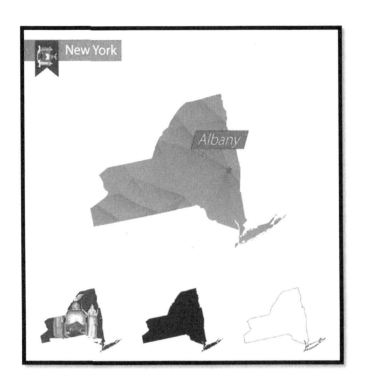

New York

Albany

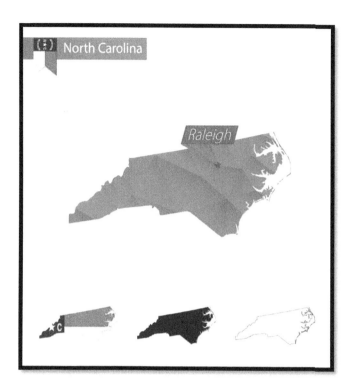

North Carolina

Raleigh

Ohio

Columbus

85

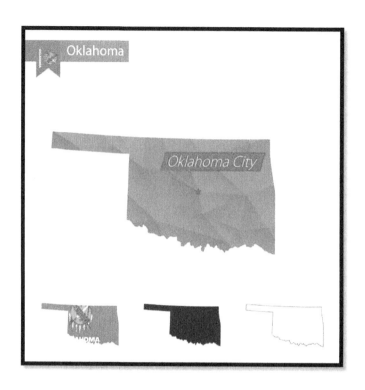

Oregon

Salem

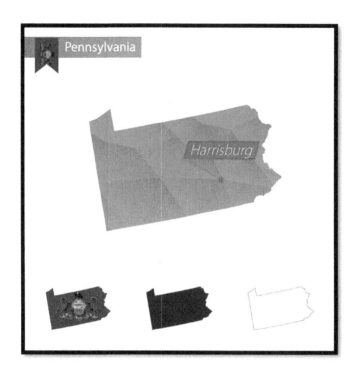

Pennsylvania

Harrisburg

88

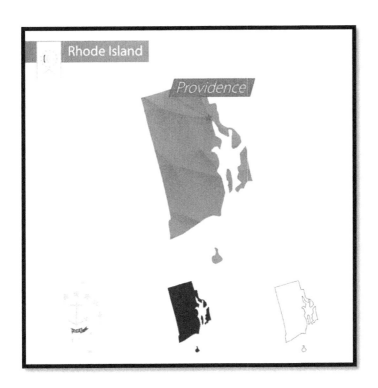

Rhode Island

Providence

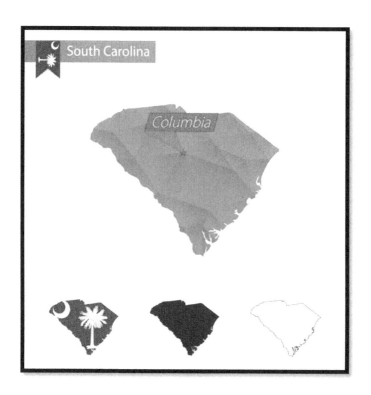

South Carolina

Columbia

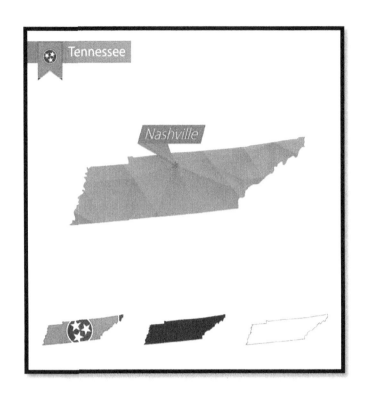

Salt Lake City

Vermont

Montpelier

West Virginia

Charleston

Wyoming

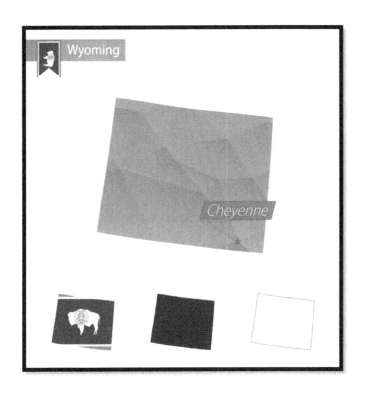

Cheyenne

Disclaimer Statement

All information and content contained in this book are provided solely for general information and reference purposes. SSP LLC Limited makes no statement, representation, warranty or guarantee as to the accuracy, reliability or timeliness of the information and content contained in this Book. Neither SSP Limited or the author of this book nor any of its related company accepts any responsibility or liability for any direct or indirect loss or damage (whether in tort, contract or otherwise) which may be suffered or occasioned by any person howsoever arising due to any inaccuracy, omission, misrepresentation or error in respect of any information and content provided by this book (including any third-party books.

Made in the USA
Middletown, DE
03 February 2023

23879361R00056